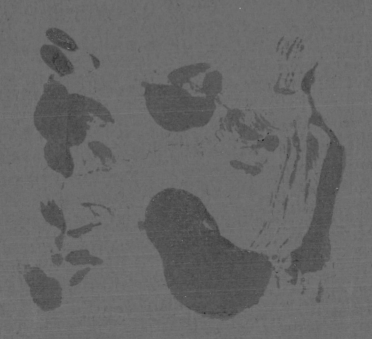

TROPICAL RAIN FORESTS
AROUND THE WORLD

TROPICAL RAIN FORESTS

AROUND THE WORLD
BY ELAINE LANDAU

Franklin Watts
New York/London/Toronto/Sydney/1990
A First Book

Library of Congress Cataloging-in-Publication Data

Landau, Elaine.
Tropical rain forests around the world / by Elaine Landau.
p.   cm. — (A First book)
Bibliography: p.
Summary: Discusses the environmental conditions of rain forests,
the plants and animals that live in these forests, and the dangers
of deforestation.
ISBN 0-531-10896-1
1. Rain forest ecology—Juvenile literature.   2. Rain forests—
Juvenile literature.   [1. Rain forest ecology.   2. Rain forests.
3. Forest ecology.   4. Ecology.]   I. Title   II. Series.
QH541.5.R27L36 1990
574.5'2642—dc20   89-24810   CIP   AC

Also by Elaine Landau

Cover photograph courtesy of
Photo Researchers (Okapia)

Map by Joe LeMonnier

Photographs courtesy of
Photo Researchers: pp. 10 (Carleton Ray), 12
(Maurice & Sally Landre), 13 (Syd Greenberg),
18 (Verna R. Johnston), 19 (Henry Engels), 23
(Gregory G. Dimijian), 24 (Verna R. Johnston),
25 (Max & Kit Hunn), 28 (Tom McHugh), 30
(Jane Latta), 34 and 35 (Kjell B. Sandved),
37 (Helen Williams), 39 (Tom McHugh), 40
(Stan Wayman), 41 (R. Van Nostrand), 43 (Tom
McHugh), 44 (Walter E. Harvey), 49 (Jonathan
Wilkins Images), 50 (Dan Guravich), 55 (top and
bottom, George Holton), 56 (Karl Weidmann).

CONTENTS

TROPICAL RAIN FORESTS AROUND THE WORLD

A WORLD
OF GREENNESS

Picture yourself in a beautiful emerald-green forest. A warm, moist, silent place. This forest looks as it did millions of years ago.

Here the trees grow tall and close together. Over 100 feet (30 m) above you, their branches and leaves join together. You're barely able to see parts of the sky. Most of the sunlight is blocked out. Only a rare beam of light breaks through to the forest floor. You might feel as though you're in a splendid green tent. Actually, you're in a tropical rain forest.

A tropical rain forest may seem like a private world of dazzling greenness. Here the leaves do not change color in autumn. They do not drop off in winter. Most tropical rain forest trees are broad-leaved evergreens. They look the same all year long.

Left: inside a tropical rain forest it is cool and dark. Temperatures in the tropics can rise to well over 100 degrees Fahrenheit. But it may be twenty degrees cooler within the forest. The moisture and lack of sunlight cool the interior. This forest in Puerto Rico is part of the Caribbean National Forest. Above: termites are among the most common insects on the forest floor. They feed on dead wood, of which there is an abundant supply in tropical rain forests. Some termites build huge nests or mounds. This dwelling houses as many as three million insects.

Inside a tropical rain forest you don't hear the rustle of a breeze. This is because the wind cannot break through the dense top leaves. So the branches below do not shake. Tropical rain forests are inhabited by many different animals. But some of them are hard to see because they usually remain hidden and silent. Tropical rain forests are dark and peaceful. They are areas of beauty and mystery.

CONDITIONS
FOR GROWTH

There are two major factors necessary for the growth of a tropical rain forest: high temperatures and a lot of rainfall. A tropical rain forest can exist only in a warm climate. The temperature must range between 70 and 80 degrees Fahrenheit (21° to 27°C) throughout the year. The trees in a tropical rain forest cannot survive cold weather. The plant life would die if the temperature dropped below 60 degrees Fahrenheit (16°C).

There are only two seasons in the tropical rain forest: the wet season and the dry season. The temperature does not change very much from day to day. Or from season to season. In fact, there isn't more than a 10-degree difference (5.5 Celsius degrees) between the hottest and coldest months of the year.

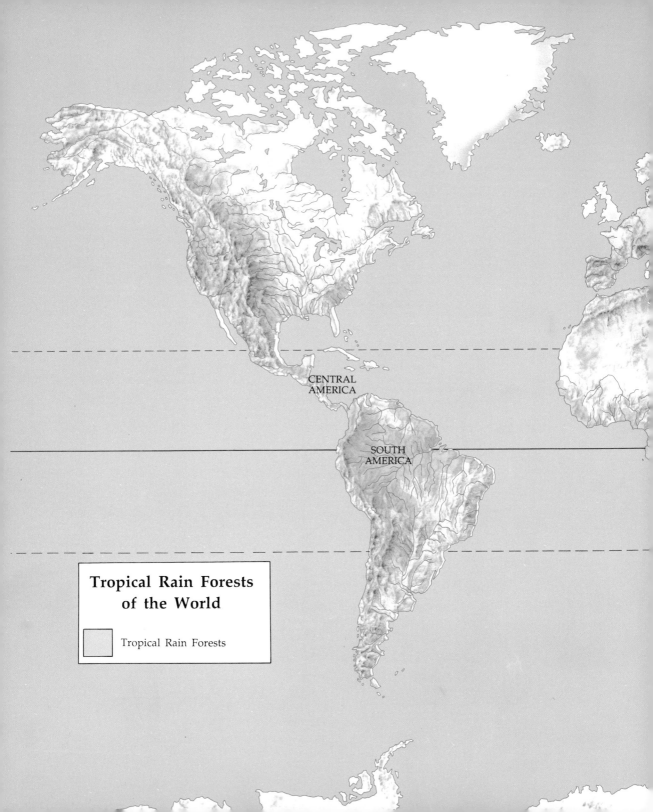

**Tropical Rain Forests
of the World**

Tropical Rain Forests

CENTRAL
AMERICA

SOUTH
AMERICA

SOUTH EAST
ASIA

FRICA

NEW GUINEA

MADAGASCAR

AUSTRALIA

Above: a tropical forest rain shower can be spectacular. There are heavy downpours. You can hear the roaring echoes of thunder. There may also be brilliant displays of lightning. However, in spite of all this rain, the forest's soil is not washed away.

Facing page: after a heavy downpour, the rain forest's soil may become muddy and waterlogged as shown here in the Cloud Forest Preserve in Costa Rica. Tropical rain forests usually do not experience flash floods.

Tropical rain forests only thrive where there is a great deal of rainfall. Heavy downpours are essential. These forests receive at least 80 inches (200 cm) of rain each year. Some tropical rain forests receive as much as 200 to 300 inches (about 500 to 750 cm) of rain annually. In the United States, many forest areas only get about an inch (2.54 cm) of rain a week. But in a tropical rain forest, it may rain over an inch in one day.

The dense forest vegetation soaks up the wetness. Later the plant leaves slowly give off the moisture. It is released back into the atmosphere. Eventually, clouds will gather and the moisture will again fall as rain.

These forests thrive in the tropics because of the area's warm, steamy weather. Tropical rain forests usually exist in places along the *equator*. The four major geographic regions in which tropical rain forests may be found are:

1. South and Central America
2. Africa and Madagascar
3. South and Southeast Asia
4. New Guinea and Australia

TREES

A typical forest in the United States contains five or six different types of trees within a given area. But a tropical rain forest is far more varied. It contains a vast mix of plant life and vegetation. Anywhere between twenty-five and over five hundred different trees may grow on a single acre.

Tropical rain forests' vegetation grows in layers or on different levels. There are no clear-cut boundaries. It may often be difficult to tell where one layer ends and the next begins.

The three levels of a tropical rain forest are the canopy, the understory, and the forest floor. The tallest level is called the *canopy*. There, trees stand between 75 and 150 feet (23 to 46 m) high. Most of the canopy trees have slender towering trunks. They branch out at the crown. The canopy forms a green forest roof of tree crowns. The forest canopy basks in the sunlight. It acts as a huge umbrella. The canopy blocks out most of the sunlight and rain from the levels below.

In some tropical rain forests, giant trees grow to a height of 250 feet (76 m). These tall trees, which poke through the forest canopy, are known as *emergents.*

Emergents look like high columns reaching toward the sky. But despite their height, these trees have very shallow root systems. Tropical rain forest trees don't send their roots very deeply into the ground. This is because the soil's *nutrients* largely remain on the surface level. The shallow root systems do not provide very much support.

As a result, some very tall trees develop buttressed roots. Buttressed roots are broad fans of extended roots. They grow out from the tree's base. These roots act as props for added support. The buttressed roots fortify the tree. They also help to balance the tree's bulk in the thin rain-forest soil.

The forest level below the canopy is called the *understory.* The understory contains a mix of small trees. There are vines and palms as well. Further down are the shrubs and very small ferns. Since the canopy absorbs most of the sunlight, the understory

Buttressed roots help to balance the tree's weight by adding support at its base. This is important as the tall tropical rain forest trees tend to have slender trunks.

Left: the cannonball tree pictured here grows in tropical rain forests. The tree sprouts flowers from its heavy bark. From the flowers, clusters of round brown fruits are produced. These clusters dangle from the tree's branches and trunk, and resemble rusty cannonballs. Above: another unusual tree found in the rain forests of Africa and the West Indies is the "sausage tree." Beautiful red flowers bloom on this tree for only a day. When the flowers fall from the tree, a sausage-shaped fruit grows in its place.

tends to be dark and humid. There's a lot of moisture in the air. Some of the trees in the understory are actually young canopy trees. These trees have not yet reached their full height.

The lowest level of a tropical rain forest is the *forest floor*. Here, herbs, mosses, and fungi live on the ground.

PLANTS

There are very few flowering plants on the floor of a tropical rain forest. This is because only a small amount of light ever reaches the ground. However, much plant life lives off the trunks and branches of trees. In this way, plants are able to reach the nourishing sunlight.

Many different kinds of vines grow in tropical rain forests. Some vines even coil themselves around an entire tree trunk. At times, the vines drape across several trees growing closely together. In this way, the vines help to support the trees against the strong tropical winds.

Lianas are a type of climbing vine. Most lianas begin as seeds on the dark forest floor. Then they

Climbing vines such as these lianas in the Mexican tropical rain forest may stretch from the forest floor to its canopy. Some grow to a length of 3,000 feet.

begin their climb up the tree's trunk. They are actually trying to reach the sunlight. A liana may grow up one tree and disappear into a thick mass of leaves. Then the vine may swoop down toward the ground again in a huge loop. Often a liana will continue its snakelike growth. It may reach out to a second and a third tree as well.

In many ways, lianas have proven useful to the people who live in tropical rain forests. The vine's stems are thick, coarse, and strong. They have been used to make bridges over wide gulfs of water. Lianas also provide a woody fiber known as rattan. Rattan has been used to make baskets. It has also been used for various items of furniture.

Many types of tropical rain forest plants grow on other vegetation. An *epiphyte,* or air plant, is a plant that thrives on the branches or trunk of another plant. The name "epiphyte" comes from two Greek words. *Epi* means "upon"; *phyton* means "plant."

Although these plants live on other plants, they do not injure their host. Epiphytes do not depend on their host for food. They take their food from the air and the wet tropical environment.

Epiphytes grow just as any plant might. They simply don't sprout up from the soil. Instead, they live in the air while resting on a tree.

There are over 20,000 different types of orchids. In tropical rain forests, orchids usually grow on tree trunks, branches, or rocks. Here orchids grow on a tree in a Colombian rain forest.

Many epiphytes are lovely flowering plants. Orchids are one example. They can be found on numerous trees in tropical rain forests.

Not all epiphytes, or air plants, are flowering plants. Ferns and mosses grow thickly on the limbs and trunks of rain forest trees. Many of these are epiphytes. A single tree may support numerous kinds of air plants. For example, orchids, ferns, mosses, and other plants may all live on the same tree.

Parasites are another form of tropical rain forest vegetation. A parasitic plant is one that is unable to live on its own. Parasites live off other plants to survive. Unlike other plants, parasites cannot manufacture their own food directly from the sunlight. Instead, parasites take their food supply from the plants they attach themselves to. Many types of tropical rain forest fungi are parasitic plants. This includes some mushrooms.

Saprophytes are still another form of tropical rain forest plant life. These plants need almost no sunlight. Like parasites, saprophytes cannot manufacture their own food. But these plants do not survive through other living plants. Instead, they attach themselves to dead organic matter on the forest floor. Saprophytes live on fallen leaves, flowers, and twigs. They also thrive on rotted wood and other decaying matter.

INSECTS

The world's tropical rain forests contain a remarkable number of insects. There may be as many as thirty million different types of insects within the world's tropical rain forests. Some types of rain forest insects may seem unusual or even extraordinary.

Many tropical rain forest insects live on the cool, dark forest floor. These insects eat forest *debris.* They feed on fallen leaves and fruits. They also eat branches, flowers, and animal excrement found on the ground.

In this way, the insects act as an able army of sanitation workers. Without them, much of the rain forest vegetation would soon be buried in its own waste.

By eating forest waste, the insects also help to break down the dead fallen matter. This releases valuable nutrients contained within the debris. Vitamins and minerals are freed. Other important elements are released also.

The insects only use a tiny portion of what is broken down. The rest of the nutrients are returned to the earth. The trees and other vegetation benefit from this process. They absorb these nutrients from the soil through their roots.

Many types of algae, ants, fungi, termites, centipedes, and earthworms may be found in tropical rain forests. They busily labor under piles of dead wood and debris. Some are so tiny that they cannot be seen by the naked eye.

Many other types of insects inhabit tropical rain forests. There are a wide range of butterflies. Various butterflies fly at different levels of the forest.

Often the butterfly's color patterns are important to its survival. Butterflies whose wings are bordered in black send an important color signal to their enemies. It is a warning that they are poisonous.

At times a butterfly's colors may serve as *camouflage.* This means that they are able to blend in with their surroundings. Camouflage helps the butterfly to conceal itself, and, therefore, serves as protection from enemies.

Here termites in the Amazon rain forest have
created a tunnel to their nest from a fallen log.
Termites help with the breakdown of wood
into soil. A million termites can rid a forest
floor of over ten tons of wood within a year.

Mosquitoes are common to tropical rain forests
as well. Many more kinds of mosquitoes exist in
these regions than in the United States. Some tropical
rain forest mosquitoes carry infectious diseases such
as malaria and yellow fever.

This brilliantly colored blue butterfly inhabits the Amazon rain forest. It feeds on the sweet nectar of rain forest flowers.

ANIMALS AND BIRDS

More types of birds and animals live in tropical rain forests than anywhere else on earth. In many ways, all tropical rain forests are similar. However, there are differences. For example, the tropical rain forests of South America, Asia, and Africa have varying kinds of similar animals.

In all tropical rain forests, some animals stay high up in the treetops. They live on the fruits and nuts found in the forest canopies. These animals may never touch the forest floor in their lifetimes.

Often these treetop dwellers are well suited to their life above the ground. One such animal is the lemur. Lemurs are furry, squirrel-size animals. They've inhabited the tropical rain forests for over

Different kinds of lemurs vary in size, markings, and appearance. The ring-tailed lemur shown here is one of the most common types. It can be found in the tropical rain forests of southwest Madagascar.

fifty million years. These agile animals travel by swinging from tree to tree. They glide through the forest at a high level.

Marmosets are monkeys found in Panama's and South America's tropical rain forests. Marmosets are often less than a foot (30 cm) long, and many have tails which are actually longer than their bodies. They weigh under a pound. Marmosets are thought to be among the smallest monkeys in the world.

Marmosets jump from tree to tree to gather food. They have long clawed fingers. These are useful for digging insects out of tree bark.

Among the largest apes living in the tropical rain forests of Sumatra and Borneo is the orangutan. An orangutan is a large animal with a hairless face and small ears. Long auburn hair covers its body.

Orangutans are impressively strong. They can grow to between 3 and 5 feet (0.9 to 1.5 m) tall, and some weigh as much as 200 pounds (91 kg). Female orangutans tend to be about half the size of the males. The orangutan's strong arms are especially important to its life in the forest. It uses its arms to climb through the forest's tree branches.

Orangutans may look fierce, but they are actually quiet, peaceful animals. Human hunters are their most dangerous enemies. Orangutans are an *endangered species.*

Orangutans live high in the trees of tropical rain forests. They stay together in small groups and build nests in the trees to sleep in. Occasionally, these large apes climb down to the forest floor.

Some anteaters have long tube-shaped heads. Anteaters have poor hearing and sight, but a good sense of touch. Their long tongues are helpful in capturing prey.

Anteaters are toothless animals with small mouths. They are common in tropical rain forests. Anteaters feed on termites and other insects. They have long hooklike claws. Their claws are useful for destroying termite nests as well as for defending themselves.

Anteaters capture their *prey* with their long tongues. Anteaters are extremely important in keeping a sense of balance in the rain forest. They help keep down the overwhelming number of termites and other insects there.

A tapir is a short, heavyset, thick-necked animal. Tapirs look like large pigs. They live in the depths of the forest regions east of South America's Andes Mountains. They are also found in Sumatra

These black-and-white Malayan tapirs are often found near riverbanks, where they feed on grasses, soft twigs, and fruits. The animals are good swimmers and enjoy cooling off in the water. Tapirs have a keen sense of smell and hearing to warn them of danger. These animals are slow to fight, but quick to flee.

and on the Malay Peninsula. Unfortunately, tapirs are still the target of hunters. Their hides are considered desirable. As a result, the number of tapirs has greatly decreased. Many other types of interesting and unusual animals live in tropical rain forests as well.

Different kinds of birds are commonly found throughout tropical rain forests. Some are brilliantly colored. Among these are long-tailed parrots called macaws. Macaws live in South America's rain forests. They are magnificent birds of scarlet, blue, yellow, green and other colors.

The macaws' beauty makes them a prized target for hunters. But these birds do not make good pets. They have powerful jaws and are fierce biters.

One of the most unusual-looking birds of the Central and South American rain forests is the tou-

Macaws, the largest parrots, nest in the holes of tall trees. About eighteen different types of these long-tailed, beautifully colored birds inhabit tropical rain forests in South America, Central America, and Mexico.

can. Toucans have large brightly colored bills. A toucan's bill may combine bands of blue, green, red, and yellow. There are over forty types of toucans.

Tropical rain forest hummingbirds are small brightly colored birds. They travel through the forest in great bursts of activity. There are over 235 kinds of hummingbirds in the tropical rain forests of South America alone. Many have strikingly colored feathers which seem to glow.

The hummingbirds that live in tropical rain forests play an important role in the reproduction of many flowering plants. The hummingbirds fly up to the flower to draw out its nectar. They keep their position in the air by rapidly beating their wings. This creates a breeze that blows pollen from one flower to the next. In this way, hummingbirds play an active role in flower pollination. Hummingbirds are the only pollinators of certain types of flowers.

Brightly colored hummingbirds feed on flower nectar and forest insects. The insects supply the hummingbirds with protein. The proteins serve as fuel for the birds' busy flight through the forest.

PEOPLE OF
THE RAIN FORESTS

Over two hundred million people live in the world's tropical rain forests. Many of them have lived in the forests for hundreds of years. Tropical rain forest people live mostly by hunting, fishing, and eating wild fruits.

In some rain forests, they live in houses made of poles and palm leaves. In other forests, the homes may be built of wood.

Some children who live in tropical rain forests do not go to school. Instead, they learn what they need for survival from their parents and other people. The children learn how to hunt deer and wild pigs and other animals. They may learn how to grow vegetables too. They learn the cries of different birds and animals. These children learn which plants and animals are dangerous and which are helpful. People who live in tropical rain forests live in harmony with nature.

WHY TROPICAL RAIN FORESTS ARE IMPORTANT

You may live thousands of miles from a tropical rain forest. But these regions play an important part in your everyday life. Have you ever eaten a chocolate bar, a banana, or a pineapple? All these foods were first discovered growing in a tropical rain forest. Now they are grown on plantations and are then shipped to markets around the world.

Most American kitchens contain many foods that come from the tropical rain forest. Among these are coffee beans, Brazil nuts, vanilla, and cinnamon. Other commonly eaten foods first came from tropical rain forests. These include corn, sweet potatoes, manioc (tapioca pudding), rice, oranges, guavas, mangoes, papayas, cashews, and chocolate.

These green coffee beans (Robusta type) are being grown in Brazil. Coffee is one of the most widely grown food crops in South America.

This is a sugarcane field in Brazil. Sugarcane is a major export crop sold overseas.

Most of our brown and white sugar is made from sugarcane. This plant was first found in tropical rain forests. In addition, the tropical rain forest sapodilla tree provides a chewy substance called chicle. Chicle is used as a base for chewing gum.

Tropical rain forests may prove to be an important source for new foods as well. A number of delicious tropical rain forest fruits may one day be found in American supermarkets. Among these is the feyoa. Feyoas are tangy pineapple-flavored fruits.

Tropical rain forests are also extremely important to doctors and medical research. Many of the drugs now sold in pharmacies first came from plants. Many plants found in the tropical rain forest have provided researchers with drugs that may help to treat some life-threatening diseases, such as cancer. Other medicines that come from plants are used to help treat headaches, skin irritations, high blood pressure, and heart disease.

The tropical rain forests of the world offer a wealth of resources. Many waxes, alcohols, flavorings, dyes, and sweeteners come from these areas. Fibers from tropical rain forests are used in life jackets, straw hats, and many rubber products. And in the future, tropical rain forests may provide new sources for fuel. Scientists think that some tropical rain forest trees produce substances which might be used to run cars and heat homes.

Tropical rain forests are especially important because they help to protect the earth's climate. When a tropical rain forest is burned, carbon dioxide is released into the atmosphere. There it absorbs much of the sun's heat. As a result, the planet warms up. Scientists have called this the *"greenhouse effect."*

If the greenhouse effect continued unchecked, global temperatures would rise. Changes in rainfall would affect crop growth. The very warm weather might melt polar ice caps. As a result, the sea levels would rise. Major coastal cities around the world would be flooded.

DANGER!

The tropical rain forests of the world are in danger. In recent years, these lush green empires are becoming scarce. People cut down trees for firewood or for lumber to build with. Tropical rain forests have also been burned or destroyed to grow food on the land or to create cattle-grazing areas.

Some governments have encouraged settlers to go into the rain forests. They've tried to move these people out of the crowded areas of their countries. Some governments have cleared portions of the forests and have offered new settlers free land, tools, and seeds.

However, often people can't survive in the tropical rain forest. The thin tropical rain forest soil is not good for growing crops. Often the land washes away almost as soon as it is cleared. This is because once the trees are gone, there is nothing to hold the soil in place during rainstorms. Large numbers of people came to the rain forests because they wanted a farm of their own. But many have been disappointed because the land is not good for growing food.

Big corporations have also plundered the forests' trees and wildlife. In some cases, the forests have been exploited for large profits. These organizations and individuals lack respect for the forests. They do not understand the true value these green wonderlands hold for us all.

More than 40 percent of the world's tropical rain forests have already been destroyed. These forests will not return in our lifetime, or maybe not even during the lifetimes of our children or grandchildren. Every year a space about the size of West Virginia is wiped away.

The clearing and burning of forests is known as *deforestation*. Each year more than a thousand types of plants and animals are destroyed by the process. The deforestation of tropical rain forests is especially tragic. This is because more types of plants and animals may be found there than anywhere else on earth.

This area of a rain forest in Guatemala was burned and cleared to plant crops. It is estimated that humans destroy nearly thirty-five acres of tropical rain forest each minute!

Once a magnificent Guatemalan rain forest, this area was cleared for farming. It is now used to grow corn.

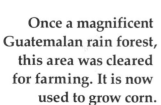

Many scientists, along with other concerned individuals, are alarmed. They believe that saving the world's tropical rain forests is one of the most important issues of our time. Deforestation must be halted. Tropical rain forests can be used to enrich all humankind. It is important to protect these forests. Their survival is crucial to our world.

This small lake in an undisturbed rain forest in Costa Rica shows nature at its most beautiful and best.

GLOSSARY

Camouflage—protective coloring that allows an animal to blend in with its natural surroundings.

Canopy—the crowns or tops of tropical rain forest trees that form a covering of leaves that shade the forest floor. The trees forming the forest canopy stand between 75 and 150 feet (23 to 46 m) high.

Debris—the remains of something broken down or destroyed.

Decay—to spoil or rot.

Deforestation—the burning or clearing of forests.

Emergents—the tallest trees in a tropical rain forest. They may reach a height of 250 feet (76 m) and extend out over the forest's canopy.

Endangered species—a grouping of animals or plants that are in danger of being completely wiped out or destroyed.

Epiphyte—(also known as an air plant); a plant that grows on another plant, but takes its nutrients from the air. Epiphytes do not harm their hosts.

Equator—the great circle of the earth that lies midway between the North and South Poles.

Forest floor—the lowest level of the tropical rain forest where herbs, mosses, and fungi grow.

Greenhouse effect—the way in which the earth's atmosphere traps the sun's heat near the earth's surface. This causes a warming effect.

Liana—a type of climbing vine.

Nectar—a sweet liquid given off by the flowers of some plants.

Nutrients—food supply for trees. Nutrients are held in the soil; when the roots of plants take in moisture in the soil from rainfall, they also take in their food supply.

Parasite—a plant or animal that lives off another living plant or animal.

Pollination—the transfer of tiny grains called pollen from the male organs of flowering plants to the female part.

Prey—any creature hunted or caught for food.

Reproduction (plant)—the process by which plants create more of their own kind.

Saprophyte—a plant that lives off nutrients in dead matter.

Understory—the forest level below the canopy that contains a mix of young trees, vines, and palms.

FOR FURTHER READING

Gould, Gill, compiler. *Animals in Danger: Forests of Africa.* Windermere, Fla.: Rourke Corporation, 1982.

Harris, Susan. *Upside-Down Creatures.* New York: Franklin Watts, 1978.

Johnson, Sylvia A. *Animals of the Tropical Rain Forests.* Minneapolis: Lerner Publications, 1976.

O'Toole, Christopher. *Discovering Ants.* New York: Bookwright Press, 1986.

Penny, Malcolm. *The Food Chain.* New York: Bookwright Press, 1988.

Ricciuti, Edward R. *Jungles.* Racine, Wisc.: Western Publishing, 1984.

INDEX